THE SECRET OF UNIVERSAL MANIFESTATION & ABUNDANCE

Contents

-Introduction-

We have no representation, either real or imagined, for the undefinable power of the Universe. Any attempt to classify, or categorize the Universe based upon our limited understanding would render it a human creation, and leave us ignorant of the truth.

No physical form can contain, or even come close to establishing a baseline of comprehension for, the never ending breadth and depth of the Universe. Infinity will never fit in a container, no matter how large you imagine it to be. Any limitation that you imagine, or attempt to impose, evaporates instantly upon release of your ego. You are in tune with, and have the potential to join, the flow of the one infinite mind which is the Universe.

There is a popular saying: "Don't believe everything you think." This is sage advice when it comes to manifesting universal abundance. The Universe IS as you are. The infinity of being nurtures any true dream of your heart, and nourishes that dream to manifestation. It already resides here and now. As you read these very words it is winking at you patiently from behind the curtain of illusion that you have constructed.

Fear and doubt often seem to paralyze the dreaming human egoic mind. They are, however, nothing more than con artists of our own creation. The moment we wake and move past our illusions, we have arrived. It does not take hard work and concentration; in fact it requires nearly the opposite. It requires surrender of the ego, and trust in our inherent wholeness. In other words you are already there, you simply might not realize it yet.

Remove from yourself the illusion that you are contained within your physical body. You are here in the infinite, timeless, now.

You are no more and no less than a complete and whole reflection of the Universe. You are flowing flawlessly in abundance, and are a mirror image of Infinity. You are the Truth.

"A spirit is manifest in the laws of the universe — a spirit vastly superior to that of man, and one in the face of which we with our modest powers must feel humble."

-Albert Einstein

Chapter 1
-Being-

The spirit loves to be, thrusting you into action based upon true inspiration. The word inspiration makes no secret of its source: in-spirit-action. When inspired you require no outside rule book or plan of action. Inspiration moves through you like waves move through the sea. To be inspired is to find what already is, without seeking. Effortless inspiration is power which comes from your heart when you allow your true self to rise above the illusions of the ego.

To do something is to go through a set of motions and emerge on the other side having completed a predetermined process. To be is to surrender to inspiration; or spirit directing you from within.

The ego loves to do. Its prize is a predetermined checklist of items to be completed, resulting in a demonstrably finished task. Our culture adores and celebrates doers. Books and instructional programs designed to improve your abilities and concentration as an effective doer abound. Doing what your ego thinks that you should be doing is the motivation of doers. "Doing this will make you a good person..." "Doing this will make you rich..." "Doing this make you attractive to a potential mate..." The list goes on and on. The problem with doing is that it leads you on a wild chase away from, or at best parallel to, the true desires of your heart.

Through doing we inhabit an illusory comfort zone where everything is preplanned and known. We may choose to do the uninspired prescribed busywork of the ego, or we may instead allow ourselves to be inspired to be who we truly are.

Through being we allow ourselves to transcend illusion and tap into the infinite source of our true spirit, which is nothing less than the Universe. This Universal manifestation is the source of our being. Inspiration is our awareness.

In being you are here, whole, and open to manifestation. In dreaming of there when you are here, you close yourself to manifestation. Dreams dwell outside of our reach- while truth never leaves our being.

"True happiness is to enjoy the present, without anxious dependence of the future"

– Seneca

Chapter 2
-Time-

Realize that everything that you think you know is an illusion. Every perceived problem is an opportunity. Every failure a gift.

Do not fall into the trap of believing that what you perceive as real is actually real. Trials, tribulations, barriers, and walls, evaporate in front of true being. No drama…no darkness…no death is real. Being is complete here and now.

Illusion must be recognized before it can be dispersed. Otherwise you may construct mountains of illusion; possibly an entire imagined alter universe. The ego may become entrenched in its effort to destroy the ego! Take care not to imagine yourself superior to, or a graduate from, the subtle tricks of illusion. What a delight to the ego to occupy any lofted space. Illusion, through pride of accomplishment, creates a vacuum of captured reflected light; away from the humility needed to stand in the infinite light.

Emerging from the dark theatre of delusion, the emergence of true light feels blinding. The temptation to remain in the theatre, instead of exiting its illusory realm into the actual, may feel strong. This pull to remain in the realm of the known and comfortable proves itself a weakling through standing and laughing at the powerless fear of the unknown (unremembered).

We need to remember not to over analyze. Now you're here, now you're there, and none of it is by accident. Everyone you meet has something to teach you. Remember now that underneath our masks there is nothing but truth. Realize that you should not act so surprised when truth shows up anywhere or everywhere; because that's where it is. That, in fact, is all there is.

We are infinitely choosing. Now we are there, now we are happy, now we are sad, now we are rich, now we are poor, now we are sick, now we are well, now the sun sets, and as always...we are right here, and right now. We are as infinite as our Universe...not the limited mind created Universe. We are always here...always now... always I AM.

Our understanding of time...right here and now...is not unlike an eye opening from a deep sleep. A dawning, ever expanding, awareness of what already is perpetually now. It is a breath filling the lungs, a sound resonating through the ears. It is the I Am experiencing the joy and wonder of its infinite wholeness.

What is there for you in the future? You may think of the future as the fulfillment of your destiny. The idea of the future may involve a mission accomplished, or a realization of a dream. The future may bring you the harvesting of the fruit that you have manifested.

The I Am is here now to tell you now that the future does not exist. The future is a fallacy; one of the grandest of illusions. The fantasies of the ego will lead you to believe otherwise. The dream of tomorrow — when everything will be better — and you will be finally happy. That tomorrow is relentlessly replaced with today. Today…with its eagerness to sink into comfortable pattern. Today…with its propensity to excuse its lack of abundance on this or that, which victimize it to its current unsatisfactory state. Today…with its hesitation, and procrastination of beginning with the first steps of wholeness. Today… Today will never cede to tomorrow. Today is you life.

Resented busyness, or wishing away tasks believed to be mundane by the ego, is a recipe for a slow baked lifetime of resistance. While the body goes through the motions of mowing the lawn, folding the laundry, taking care of others, etc; the mind fights every step of the way. Wishing things were different, lamenting that we went here instead of there, all the while watching helplessly as the decades pass. Until one day the reflection in the mirror is aged with lines of regret.

Perhaps a recognition dawns in the eyes that this lifetime has become nearly wished away. Perhaps that is what you were here to learn, and if so…mission accomplished. Or, perhaps midway through, an epiphany jars you awake to the blessings found in this very moment.

What is it that you think of when you desire to manifest? Is it a present moment here and now, or is it a future life for yourself where everything will be happier? While you sit at your table sharing a meal with a loved one, you may discuss a plan for the future. Does this future plan blend harmoniously into the here and now?

Instead, perhaps you become enamored with the dream of this future plan where you will manifest a "better life". What about the loved one sitting across from you at the table? Are they truly a loved one? If so they are the embodiment of a future that you manifested for yourself. What about the food you are using to nourish your body? What is more important than nourishment of your body with the food you choose?

Are you allowing the dream/ illusion of your future plan/ manifestation to rob you of this moment? This moment of nourishment is your life. Focus on this moment, and find freedom as dreams and illusions fall away. Then actively engage with your loved one in gratitude, while you build a fluid foundation through continuous actions. Watch as the here and now infinitely continue to manifest.

The illusory life is nothing more or less than a stage of your choosing. Players and dramas which you have selected; all in fun and learning. Underneath the pain and joy, the comedy and tragedy, is your true being…watching as the scene plays out just as planned.

This revelation may anger your ego. You may say: "I worked hard to get where I am in this life." or, "You have no idea what I have suffered." Yet our victories and defeats are choices and not chances . You are in fact reading this book because this is a transitional phase within the outline you have created for this lifetime. You are here now (as always) to begin manifesting a new scene.

If you are ready now it will be quite impossible for you not to manifest everything that you have chosen for this life. Reality has no doubts. Reality offers nothing to win, or lose. Do not worry about messing it up, because there is no worry in reality, and there is no messing up. Reality simply IS.

Your imagination exists at your permission. Your true self requires no imagination, because it is nothing less than infinite mind. So the limits of your imagination are as illusory as your ego.

Take a moment to imagine everything in the Universe. Now let go of that picture in your imagination, and realize that infinite perfection (reality) is far more beautiful, and perfect. This real universe exists well beyond your imagination, and the limits that you have decided to put upon it.

Everything that is, already was. Everything that will be, already has been. Yet everything is constantly changing, right now.

Our experiences are like a handfuls of sand. We are able to maintain them briefly. With care we can hold on quite a while. Trying to hold on too tightly inevitably causes them to slip away faster than if we relax the hand, and allow the sand to rest, as in a saucer. Either way, the sand is not ours to possess; it is only ours to experience for a brief interval. When it it falls it does not die of course. Instead, it returns to the beach, and blends right back in to where it was before. It may be scooped up again, or it may not. But it is always there, indestructible as ever.

Your true self did not design a boring lifetime for you in which your wishes instantly manifest without first the work being done, and the lessons learned. Unless, of course, the unworthiness of the wish becomes the lesson.

Now release your imagination, and recall the moments in this lifetime when you have felt reality. Perhaps it was at a moment of perceived danger, when you felt that you may "die" and were not yet ready. At such moments we can easily remember our true selves, and slow the illusion of time, in order to put things right.

We may exhibit skills or strength which our egos (and science) believe impossible. Miracles? Sure, but also part of the script, and lessons, designed for this lifetime.

Our only limitations are egoic illusions. Reality knows no illusion. How can the unreal ever contain the real? You already know that is a ridiculous question.

It has become popular to state: "I do not chase...I attract." In reality you have nothing to attract, as the Universe is you. You are not a magnet afloat in a vast universe. You are the I AM of the Universe. The whole show is yours to do with as you please. Love, light, and happiness are not, therefore, found anywhere other than within. You do not need to attract them to you because they already are you.

"There is nothing either good or bad, but thinking makes it so."

– William Shakespeare

Chapter 3
-Good and Bad-

The darkness of infectious illusion, propagated by designed campaigns of divisive groupthink, act not unlike a hurricane. Starting as a harmless bit of low pressure, a groupthink infection can begin to spin faster and faster, and pick up more and more moist hot air, until it resembles a powerful truth. What's black is white, and white is black; according to the illusory biases of our chosen tribe.

All of a sudden we are deluded to believe that there is true good, and true evil. We are pitted against the other in a relentless hailstorm of falsehood and predigested opinion. You are with us, or against us. No middle ground. Clinch a fist and raise it in the air for your side.

Now quickly unclinch that fist and open your eyes. Look closely upon the "other" you are spun to hate. Examine her family, see him smile at his child. Understand your similarities (which are abundant). Remember that we are all one. Release anger, and allow recognition of true spirit.

No amount of physical strength, brute force, weaponry, or financial resource will bring about manifestation. The largest bank account is rendered impotent upon check out from an illusory, egoic existence. The true desires of the heart are not for sale, and they can not be stolen. Force is a farce in the face of truth.

Be as you are. Do not fear missteps, or consequences. You are whole, and there are no mistakes. It is as it has been: neither good, bad, right, nor wrong. Rules and laws are fine if you want them; but they have nothing to do with what Is.

It is easy to trust our egoic beliefs about what is good and proper behavior relating to the choices of "others". Would your higher power truly require your assistance? Have you been deputized by the Universe to impose what you understand to be correct unto others?

We are inter-connectedly on our own journey within the woven perfection of the Universe. It may be necessary to separate the violent from the society; but do not confuse this with moral superiority. There is a here and now where the accepted collective choices of your society are considered violent.

Do not cling to laws and egos as the defining substance of what is good, bad, right, or wrong. Unclasp these illusory ideas to taste the freedom which the universe has provided.

You may wish to believe that only the innocent, true, and just, may manifest the desires which come from a pure heart. Would you count yourself among this number? Would you decide as to the other whose heart you believe to be impure?

What separation is there between you and this perceived other? What truths do you possess that they do not? What path of the righteous do you follow, compared to what you believe to be their path of the fallen? What reward do you imagine for yourself? What peril for them?

What laws have you passed to reinforce your illusions? What punishments have you deemed fit for those who fail to heed your command? What authority have you anointed upon your ego to delegate, and relegate? This is good and that is bad? This is pure and that is evil? This is true and that is false?

You have set your sails to follow the superior breezes of the deluded. Your self (egoic) decided path of righteousness is as much delusion as the alternative perceived path of the damned. Both paths lead nowhere, as both are fictitious creations of the ego.

The Universe has no care for what the ego believes to be right or wrong. As you sit in judgment, therefore, begin to unravel and see things from a thoughtless perspective. As such, allow in the knowing that you can not be right, and you can not be wrong. You may simply be. In being, you are one with Infinity.

To judge another is to judge yourself. We are grown and fed from the same root. So do not think about how others perceive you. They are you, and you them. If another is removed from society for violent actions, understand that their actions, and subsequent isolation, are equal among all. Thinking one to be righteous, while another is wicked, is the prize of vain ego.

The Isness of love requires no box, or
definition. Truth is not swayed by human thought.
The fictitious you is in no way separate from the
fictitious other. That you declare some as "good
and right," and others as "wrong and gone astray,"
provides such a satisfying pleasure for the ego!
But such egoic thought of course leads you
nowhere other than its own dream state, which has
absolutely nothing to do with impenetrable truth.

So when the ego is employed in the creation
of law and order, do not yield to its illusory
temptations. What illusion erects as a pillar of
normalcy is no more than a misguided hand held
up in an attempt to block the wind; or a pebble
placed in an attempt to dam the sea. The universe
is in no need of human law. Universal laws require
no enforcement, or punishment. There is no
audience judgement. There are no rules to break.
Just you: Here and eternally now.

Perhaps you are concerned for the morality of those whom you think are outside from, or different than yourself. Maybe you concern yourself with "saving" souls you believe are separate from your own. You would then presume yourself to be "right," or to be possessor of some magic rulebook upon which you may reference to assist others in their morality. There will always be an abundant supply of contradictory magic rule books; yet only One soul (which is not in need of saving).

The atonement of the way showers is within. It is no more or less than a reflection of the one mind, accessible to you always. The Universe does not need you to defend it. Think about that for a moment. The Is, the All, Love…whatever you want to call the I Am within you, knows nothing other than perfection. Any desire you may feel to lead others towards salvation is one of the grandest, and silliest, illusions of the ego. You do not need to repent to the Universe which knows no mistakes.

Learn to laugh at fear. There is nothing that can harm you. Do not linger long over the outrage those words inspire in the ego. Control over the unseen is the desire of the ego. Detachment from the ego is the happy Infinite song of the Universe.

It's all in the way that we choose to look at what's in front of us. What we see is what we get. Of course what we see may have nothing to do with the truth. If we choose fear, then we see frightening illusions which can seem very real indeed. But fear is purely a choice that we make. There is absolutely no need for fear. Truth is all that there is, and there is no fear in truth. Like turning on a light switch in a dark room—suddenly that which is not there, is revealed to not be there. All of the monsters, and boogey men created in illusion are exposed as nothingness.

When you choose to focus on nothing other than that true song of the Universe, illusion melts away. The music requires no cares in the world other than its beautiful direction, wild untamed possibility, and perfect flow.

In truth we have no place for fear, or evil, or any other such illusion. When we realize that we are an unalterable reflection of truth, we see that there is no beginning, no ending, no middle, and no mistakes. Only truth, and no matter the false trials we create for ourselves, we can't mess it up. There is no good and bad, no right and wrong, only truth.

We see through our delusions the end of light, the closing of a book, the cessation of being; but none deter truth. As seductive as illusion can seem, it fades to nothingness the instant that truth comes into focus.

Waves unfolding on the sand-
fist released revealing hand.
Anger is present, festering, hot-
but truth is real and anger not.
Love is lurking--no
ABOUNDING unseen.
It is real, pure, and clean.
Paper bills and precious metals-
Neither found in a flowers petals.
But LOVE is there as I as you.
Tears of joy like morning dew.

Chapter 4
-Money-

Human dreams and illusions of grandeur---
of having more, or having less-- of the wealthy,
and the poor, fade upon the bright light of being.
We are as I AM; and we are whole and eternal.
Our dreams may plunge us to depressive depths;
and they may send us soaring to elite heights. But
they are nothing but dreams. They are whimsical
fancy, given form by an illusory understanding of
mind, spirit, and all that truly is here and now.

The Universe does not know the value of
silver or gold. It does not know the power
misguidedly placed upon paper currency, or pixels
on a screen, designed to establish worth.
Worthiness is not for sale or barter. Worthiness is
intrinsic in all which make up the Universe. Value
is equally spread, and accessible, throughout the
oneness of all that is.

This understanding arrives, not unlike
waking and opening your eyes to a ray of sunlight
in the room. But now the question: Can this state
be achieved equally by one who possesses money,
and by one who does not? Is it not immeasurably
easier to feel at one with the Universe when you do
not have empty pockets? This would seem a
paradox, as nature certainly places no value upon
human currency. Perhaps it is in the security of
knowing that you have the power, and financial
leverage, to "control" your reality through the use
of money. Maybe money allows you the luxury to
relax sufficiently to finally feel at-one-ment with
the sun's rays; and meditative visions. This seems
fraudulent. Would a true master require a full
pocket to atone? Indeed she would certainly shun
such false freedom.

You may wish to manifest money. You may
describe this wish as : abundance, freedom, and
happiness. Now contemplate whether abundance,

freedom, and happiness can be purchased with money? Money may inadvertently build an illusory persona for you to comfortably imprison yourself, before finally realizing that it provided the opposite of freedom.

You may squander much of your life saving and defending your monetary riches. Is this the freedom that you seek through your attempt to manifest money? Perhaps your desire to manifest money stems from your fear. Fear of the illusory tomorrow, with its fraudulent call for hoarding resources in order to feed, clothe, and house yourself... while the unprepared freeze, or starve outside of your doors.

In our society we are focused on money. Through illusion we have invented starvation, famine, and gluttony! This is simply fear propagating itself in an endless unsatisfiable cycle.

The time is now to let go of the reins of the fake horse, and leap from the carousel of illusion into the unknowable realm of surrender. Fear is a prison, surrender is freedom.

True abundance is not found in the hoarding of resources. Whether it be millions in the bank, or stockpiling excesses while turning a blind eye to those who have none. Abundance is a trust that there is plenty for all provided by the Universe.

Let go of the fear that you will perish. Of course your egoic idea of yourself will perish. Of course your physical body will decay. This can not be stopped through hoarding; and it is nothing to fear. This ego death, and bodily destruction. has already occurred. The hands you use to hold this book have already returned to dust in the timeless now. You, however, are also and infinitely here and now.

True manifestation, therefore, is not a mere wish for money, or possessions. Universal manifestation, quite simply, is love. Finding the motivation to manifest into your surroundings not only that which will bring yourself sustenance; but also that which is of benefit to your surroundings is the first step. You will begin to easily manifest abundance when you find the motivation for work which brings you into the harmonious song of the universe.

You will know this work from the joy that it brings. What you produce through this work will be nothing less than a product of ego free love. And through this production you will naturally begin to manifest the life of your dreams.

The manifestation of happiness is not unlike a garden that you envision and create within a patch of overgrown land. The toil you endure in clearing the land of roots, briars, and weeds is a removal of your ego from the land. This involves showing respect to the roots and other obstacles as you analyze the best way to effectively remove them. Once your patch of land is cleared, you must plow the soil; overturning illusory belief systems to allow the moist soil of understanding below to rise.

The seeds sewn into your plowed plot of earth are rows of misery, joy, pain, comfort, heartache, blessings, and regret you have known. As your seeds germinate, and you weed out distraction, you watch in awe as your plants begin to grow. The buds of your dawning understanding flower and form equally beautiful from each seed.

You pick a fruit and behold its perfection. You have known the glorious pain and ecstasy of the universe, and both reside within you in happy perfection.

The exchange of love and respect among those awakened to the song of the Universe is true abundance. True abundance is free from greed, and conversely, free from lack. An overfull stockpile of goods ironically provides its owner with lack. In such cases fear masquerades as wealth.

Putting your egoic mind, and fragile physical form, into extravagant comfort through the collecting of the false wealth of excess will unceasingly bring to you the polar opposite of the happiness, and satisfaction, which you seek. Excess is not wealth. Extravagance is not wealth. Luxury, and grandiosity are not wealth. Love is wealth.

Happiness is certainly not bought, sold, or even possessed. Abundance is the air that you breathe…Freedom is letting go…Happiness is surrender.

Let your home be your
mast and not your anchor.

-Kahlil Gibran

Chapter 5

-Shelter-

You will realize that your being, the I Am, did not originate with the joining of your physical parents. I Am was before you were this physical form; and will remain long after your current form is but a shell on the beach of the universe. See a house as nothing more than a shell built for a shell. Realize the home where you truly reside is here, now, always.

The home of your illusory dreaming may be a stunning mansion, or perhaps a simple cottage with a covered porch. Either way, understand that the construction of the home you wish to manifest begins nowhere other than your true heart. You will be able to conceive of where you are, and what you are, which is nothing less than the Universe.

Inseparable oneness is your core. Therefore your manifestations are infinitely abundant and available on the other side of dreaming. Do not veer into the delusion of worry. To worry is to reject the oneness of infinity, and to imagine yourself separate, and always in danger of falling. No such danger exists.

You will not manifest anything that is not meant for you, so disallow your thoughts from this false idea of ego. Allow your true self to simply be. Doing so is sufficient to come into alignment with all that is available to you. All that is available to you is everything.

Abundance, such as good health, joy, and a satisfied knowledge of overarching wealth, are never created. While the ego is aghast at such a statement, it is simultaneously brushed aside by its truth. Such abundance is in infinite supply right now, as always, simply waiting for you. Letting go of the busy work of delusion allows you to find it, and welcome it as your truth.

The love for all living creatures is the most noble attribute of man…

-Charles Darwin

Chapter 6
-Food-

In order to become one with abundance you must love and care for this physical form you are inhabiting. In our current societies we are programmed, and marketed to by overlarge corporations operating to generate the highest possible profit. What has been sacrificed in this process is the spirit of the food being prepared for consumption.

The stripping of the food to enable it to be processed at the cheapest cost, robs the consumer of the original spirit inherent in the harvested crops. What is left is mostly empty calories enhanced with sugar, salt, "natural", and artificial chemical flavorings in proportions designed to stimulate our brains into pleasure, and the desire for more product.

The choice of whole organic foods is a vital component of the awakening process. When holding a product you are considering for purchase, and consumption ask yourself: What is the original source of this food? How much processing has the original food source undergone to arrive at the product I am holding in my hand?

Food is the fuel for our being here and now. The spirit inherent in the food feeds the spirit within our bodies. Spirit begets spirit. As such, keep in mind the spiritual well being of your food sources.

Did the food source originate from a fellow sentient being? If so, are you sure that the dominion held over that being provided her with the opportunity to experience the pleasures of this world? The sunlight, fresh air, space to walk and be? Was the being free of human abuse? Did the being live in fear, or peace? And most importantly would you yourself be willing to slaughter the being with your own two hands and prepare her body for a place upon your plate?

"A disciplined mind brings happiness."

-The Buddha

Chapter 7
-Ego-

The infinite Universe is not constrained by any physical, or mental limitations. As such, there is no way for us to comprehend its power through our limited current level of understanding. Such human desire to place any parameter of form, limit, or even real comprehension of the Universe, will fall short. The only focus of our comprehension should be through meditation, and acceptance of our place within the oneness of all that is.

You may cling to the false notion that you are your thoughts. Nothing could be further from the truth. You are The Thought. The busyness of your thinking mind has nothing to do with the perfection of your true presentation here and now: The absolute unerring infinite realization of spirit inside of you: the I Am.

The doubts and miscalculations of the over busy thinking mind buzz around not unlike a fly circling a saucer. These distractions are but straw men, ready to be blown into oblivion by the flow of the source of all that is. As if waking from a dream, we may now open our eyes to the perfect light and oneness of eternal, indestructible, being. Allow the chatter of the thinking mind to evaporate into the happy flow of the Universe; which is found abundantly within ourselves.

Awareness is a beautiful thing. You look at your hand every day, and then one day you look at it again in a new light. What a wonderful thing it is to be alive, and free. There is no other way to be. Illusion, countered by illusion, will only lead to more illusion. To break free of oppression you have to learn to see through it, like it's not even there — because it's not.

The ego seeks illusory power, whether it's through money, fame, sex, or whatever false status it may construe. All the while true power is right here, right now waiting for you to take whenever you are ready to see things as they are. Money, sex, fame, status...they all pile up to a mountain of nothing...poof they're gone because they never were.

Are you making yourself a slave of your own thoughts? Are you a slave to your perceptions? If not then stand in the sun and acknowledge your forever-ness now! When we are awake, we are all power, all freedom. Truth is the only real formula for freedom. When we finally decide that we don't want to be slaves, and break the chains we've bound ourselves with; that's when the sweet song of being, played throughout eternity will fill our ears, and the divine taste of freedom will reach our lips!

Music is a pure form of truth, much too beautiful and vast to be contained even within imagination. Of course, it's not always an easy thing to be around. The truth is not a popular concept with the ego. It threatens those who love the persona (illusion), built by ego. Someone in this delusional state may have "built" there whole lives around misunderstandings. When they run into the truth they get upset, and ready to fight; ready to defend those misunderstandings that they've grown so fond of, and comfortable with in illusion.

To look upon an object of desire, one that you may say that you wish to manifest, as an outside creation is illusion. To say: "I wish that I may become that," or "I wish I may come to possess an object that I do not possess now," is no more than an unwinnable game of the egoic mind. You may wish, and wish, but you will certainly never receive what you wish for as a gift from the universe.

"The mind is not a vessel to be filled but a fire to be kindled."

- Plutarch

Chapter 8
-Teaching-

You do not read this book, or any other
book, in order to fill your physical brain with
knowledge that it did not previously possess. You
read this book just as you seek other answers.
What you are seeking is the memory of wholeness.
The answer is the dissipation of the illusion of
ignorance. You are as the Universe is; and your
knowledge and wisdom are complete. They are
waiting for you here and now.

Beware a teacher offering to provide you
with something lacking in your awareness. Many
who profess to teach Truth are the same which
have built mountains of illusion fueled by human
ego. When you yourself feel the drive to teach
something to another, first make yourself aware
that the drive you are feeling is indicative of your
own true lack of understanding. Your ego wants to

build its own reality, and demonstrate the
correctness of that which is actually nothing more
than illusion.

Surrendering the ego, and its need to be
right, is a sign of tremendous growth away from
the false and towards awareness. The ego
will, of course, try to take charge of that process as
well. In such a case simply acknowledge the ego,
accept its attempt, then watch as it dissolves in the
face of simple being.

The best teachers are the ones that you
hardly realize are there. This is because they
awaken in you the love of learning (remembering).
Such a teacher can remind you of the realms of
knowledge available to you within yourself.
Unlike an empty vessel in need of filling, you are
infinity.

Take no pride, and accept no shame.
Neither is known to the Universe. If an illusion of

unfairness, or false blame arises let it fester in the sunlight of truth until it bursts. Take no solace in occupation or responsibilities—indeed there is no more tempting a distraction from what is real than hiding behind the self importance of responsibilities.

Beware the sellers of salvation. Would you believe a messiah or teacher to be true who would sell you an awakening in a seminar for an admission price of $695? Of course not! The true teacher would turn over the table of such a fraud. Even if the fraudulent teacher believes themself to be true; this is a reflection of ego.

A delusional ego would lead them to respond to, and dismiss any criticism with a smugly superior and insincere "you're right." A true teacher has no desire for luxury autos, mansions, or first class travel. Attraction to such a teacher is indicative of a reflection of your own illusions.

If you believe that salvation is akin to
luxury, or freedom is found in first class airline
tickets, you are treading the waters of delusion.
Such delusion, that which believes it righteous to
jet your physical body around the globe and call it
freedom, is nothing more than vanity. Such vanity
leaves the traveler impoverished, no matter the
large sums within their money accounts.

Do not speed past the laborers of the field
on your way to the sunsets of the coast. Do not
isolate yourself in first class comfort, and view the
visited culture from behind the veil of your plastic
credit card. If you are called on to travel, go with
an open heart and immerse yourself into the visited
culture. The freedom of the universe is available
to you here and now.

How boring the movies would be without
villains. So each, in our turn, may choose to wear
the black hat. A conspiracy of friendship reaching

here and now, throughout all of our lessons. Your
perceived enemy is your great teacher, and you
theirs. Across playful bridges, always leading to I
Am, we are free to hash out dramas, and fall in
love. Heartbreak, tragedy, and triumph all swim
together in the sea of our oneness; each as the
other returning and returning lovingly to where we
have always been: right here, and right now.

So feel the sting. Come to your breaking
point, then bend a bit further. If you break, just
tuck into the dive, and emerge laughing, and
learned. Lean into the desperate, culling emptiness
of betrayal, and loss. Let the carnal desire burn a
hole right through your skin. Always then finally
remember that you are here now, and you are not
in any danger.

TRUTH =

SPIRIT =

LOVE =

UNIVERSE =

ABUNDANCE=

NOW.

Chapter 9
-Recognizing Resistance-

You have nothing to create. You have nothing to attract. There is no division, nor separation; all is inclusive, and whole. You, as an integral part of the universe, may now strongly and clearly proclaim : "I Am." There is no other way to be.

You may dream yourself to be less. You may dream yourself to be more. Upon awakening, you remain as you ever are. I Am. Here, now, forever; all three of these at once, which is eternity.

In a dreaming state of illusion there will falsely appear divisions, and separations. Such dreams paint a fictitious world of cruelty, and greed. Struggle and illness intertwine with doubt

and fear, to tempt us to cower within the confines
of the most comfortable home (tomb of the living)
that our status, and money, can buy.

Awakened from the dream, you will find
stillness, along with an awareness beyond your
vocabulary. Any struggle, strife, or resistance
evaporates into the stillness of I Am. The idea,
seed, sprout, plant, fruit, and continuing seed are
complete, whole, and immediately manifested
together as one.

The illusion of the problems of life arise
from from a short sighted view of ones place in the
Universe. To be here, now, and aware, requires
nothing less than perfect Universal oneness. From
the sunlight to the water. From the soil, to the tree,
to the fruit, to the seed. From the cell, to the
human.

You are the Universe. You are not alone or
an island. What we mistakenly label past and

future are eternally now and forever one with the always changing interdependent Universe. Making peace with the impermanence of physical form, and detachment from egoic self creates the opening required to move beyond delusion, and into true reality.

There is an old anecdote asking which is larger, the imagination or the Universe. The answer given was the imagination, in that it contained the universe! If there ever was an example of the human ego run astray this would be it. The imagination can no more contain the universe than an aquarium can contain the sea.

The imagination is but a dream. To even glimpse the true Universe one must detach from the imagination, and surrender the ego.

Let go of any vain attempt to control anything. Instead, surrender to the overwhelming feelings inherent in this life. Suffer the pain, exclaim the joy, scream the anger, weep the sadness, and cherish the ecstasy. When you have experienced these feelings, immediately release them; never cling.

Standing at the crossroads of integrity and despair, choose to follow a different path. As you are not judged by the Universe, there is no true distinction between integrity and despair. Thoughts are the police of illusion. You may choose to allow them to arrest you, or you may blow them away as the scattered seeds of a dandelion. However, unlike the dandelion, the false seeds of human thought will not sink into the earth and flower. Thoughts will immediately dissipate in the sunlight of judge-less universal oneness.

Do not speak of the faith which lies within the confines of your understanding. You have no details to offer as to the ways of the Universe. If you are to speak on faith, speak only on that which leads you to melt effortlessly into that which you do not know. The knowledge of such surrender is faith enough to move mountains.

Illusion within a group may masquerade as security through common acceptance of the false, as within an echo chamber. Talk and chatter repeated, and accepted as settled fact, robs one of self reflection and understanding through the true self. Subordinating the inner voice to the authoritative tone of an outside pseudo authority creates a treadmill of egoic laziness.

Talk for the sake of talk leads nowhere other than distraction. Such small talk serves as nothing more than a block of your channeling what

actually is. Fear, the greatest of illusions,
incessantly attempts to propel you from the
solitude which may lead to insight. When this
occurs, welcome the fear as your old friend. Greet
it, acknowledge it, and then place it away in a
corner to dispel into nothingness as you move on.

Great is the temptation to yield to the
understanding of another, whether that other be
presented in the spoken word or through writing.
Teachers are invaluable only so long as they are
propelling your insight forward. The dictation of
truth as settled unimpeachable fact, however,
provides no room for the fruitful search within.
Just as the universe continues to expand, so must
our insight.

The channelling of truth that you are
capable of moves you beyond anything written, or
spoken. Indeed, you may find no words sufficient
to describe the insight received through a quiet,

surrendered state of being. Words written, or spoken, from such a surrendered state will unfailingly flow from the true space within your heart, and may be received as a loving gift instead of a structured lecture.

The ongoing conclusion of inevitability lies fallaciously within egoic groupthink. Like a river heading relentlessly toward the sea, we imagine our lives to be heading relentlessly from birth toward death. That is an unquestionable fact of existence you may say. Now question whether you truly believe that you possess the ability to declare anything as an unquestionable fact.

The smug ego perhaps has a doctorate in delusion from the top human university; yet it labels its possessor a fool upon thinking its knowledge is unimpeachable fact. Drop the question, and delight in the miracle of being. Dismiss the ego, and allow yourself to become one with it all. The ego wants to know, define, possess, posture, create, destroy, an above all defend. Yet none of those are real.

Your ego may pretend that it is the image and likeness of the universe; or to say it another way, it, and other human egos, are the image and likeness of a God. Dispelling this delusion allows us to accept that we, in our current chosen form, are not equipped to see, hear, and comprehend everything that is happening around us. We are one with, and an integral part of, the Universe while visiting this three dimensional existence.

Letting go of the responsibility of being Godlike ourselves frees us to simply be. It allows us to come into rhythm and flow with our place within all that is. Just as we are not alone on earth, and share it with other sentient beings, plants and lifeforms down to the cellular, it is not our place to dominate. At best, we are stewards of that which we are capable of comprehending.

Illusion may ask: "Do we die?"

Does the sun set?

Illusion: "Yes."

Really?

Illusion: "Yes… every night."

Does it now?

Illusion: "No, I guess it doesn't really set, it just appears to because our Earth is turning."

Ah.

Illusion: "So we don't die?"

Does the sun set?

Illusion disappears.

Fear not when energy transfers. Energy can not be destroyed. You are energy.

Chapter 10
-Programming-

When you turn on your television to watch a program, you are voluntarily allowing your television to program to you. Allowing yourself to sit in front of a screen and be programmed brings about limitation. Comprehend the fact that the images, words, sounds, and frequencies coming out of your set are designed not only to entertain you, but to limit you as well.

When you regularly place yourself in front of such programming, you are allowing your ability to tap into the actual source of universal creativity to bow down to the repeated sequences of recycled thought patterns. By tuning out of the prescribed limitations, and social norms being force fed through programming, you will begin to settle.

When you unplug everywhere, you naturally
begin to identify with Universal frequencies.
Through the simple act of deprogramming from
media, your growth becomes limitless.
Unplugging allows you to realize that you have
been thinking thoughts designed for you by others.

Suddenly you are free by simply opening
yourself to a vast, ever-changing, creative
Universe. Can you imagine the awakening that
would occur if we were all to unplug our
televisions, and stop mindlessly surfing the
Internet? It would be a spectacular awakening to
equity.

We could immediately shine a light upon
the brutality of hoarding resources. We could
stand up, and no longer tolerate the unfairness of
exploitation. We could expose the ridiculousness
of poverty! The Universe provides abundance. We
have the power to unplug from deluded
programming, and manifest what is already ours.

Meditation is to be aware of every thought and of every feeling, never to say it is right or wrong but just to watch it and move with it. In that watching you begin to understand the whole movement of thought and feeling. And out of this awareness comes silence…

-Jiddu Krishnamurti

Chapter 11
-Meditation-

To manifest is not to bring unto yourself that which you lack. To manifest is to remove the veil of illusion, and remember that the whole of Universe is already yours. The state of abundance is your natural state. Cowering under the delusion of lack brings false states of wanting. The ego is undoubtedly screaming at this page regarding the lack of respect the above statement provides to the "injustices" of this world.

Take this egoic outrage into meditation, and reflect upon that which you imagine needs your control and blessing. Make an effort to set your ego aside, and look within onto the journey that you are on. Trust that the universe requires neither your blessing, nor your understanding. You are on a journey here, now, and always. Sit still and be.

In order to realize your manifestations, simply be. Exchange rumination for meditation. See the essence of your being within all that is. Know that there is no separation between you and the universe; and realize that you already are in possession of the true desires of your heart. Surrender the art of thinking from the illusory ego to the impenetrable heart.

Your heart knows no boundaries, or separations. Your heart knows abundance, and is the key to the universe. The only law which is impossible to break, is that of your heart. As free as you may feel, you will, and must obey. Turning, and turning, and turning, all at once into this heart which is here, and now.

Meditation will not change the universe, but it will bring us into harmony with it. Remember that you are not asking the Universe to change itself. The Universe is already perfect. You are asking the Universe to help you to match its frequency, and flow. Manifestations for all sentient beings are already flowing freely from the Universal source. The Universe is perfection, and we have no insight to offer that which is already perfect. The I Am of the Universe is free flowing, and unaware of any restraints, such as our limited human understanding of space and time.

During meditation repeat the following phrases:

I Am the Universe
I Am Love
I Am light
I Am peace
I Am joy
I Am infinite
I Am one with eternity

The life that you seek
awaits in a fog of illusion.

A November crossroads in
a timeless Universe.

Chapter 12
-Ego Death-

The only death that you must ever suffer is the death of the ego.

Your illusions may require destruction through nothing less than complete upheaval of what you, to this point, have considered your normal existence. The temptation of alcohol, and other intoxicants, may drive you to constantly escape until, at long last, the period of escape becomes more and more brief; and the consequence of the intoxicant use becomes more unbearable than the seemingly insurmountable original pain of the delusion.

Your ego will hang on, even through excruciating pain. Often it requires an unimaginable amount of pain for us to finally be rid of illusion.

Your ego will try hard to keep up the charade of the character it has constructed. It will claw into its illusory world, clinging so tightly that it may attempt to proceed to suicide as the only way out! The false fight of these delusions may indeed grind you to the point of temptation to prematurely end your physical existence as a means of escape. At this point the delusion is nearly extinguished.

This breaking point is where your ego can no longer function. This is the parting of the clouds in which the beauty of your true self can at long last laugh at the ridiculous turmoil of the ego in its resplendent nothingness.

At this moment you rise with the one who has always been with you, your true being. Oneness overwhelms the last gasps, and pathetic clamoring, of the false self which was your ego. You remember eternal love and its absolute, beautiful, indestructible, being.

In my personal experience, I can report that I could not stop laughing. Just moments before, the false grip of the ego had me considering extinguishing the breath from this form I am experiencing. Now, sweet now, I Am prepared for everything.

Upon escape from the dark curtain of the ego, you may believe yourself the possessor of new knowledge. You may feel wise, and free. Set down this resurrected ego into a suitable playpen.

As desperate as your illusory anguish under the false grip of the ego; the peace you remember upon its dissipation is infinitely more powerful. The window is always open. Love and oneness is the manifestation that you can never escape through the delusions of the ego. You are right now the one true manifestation, and nothing that you do or think can change that.

You shockingly find yourself free from
nonsense. What seemed like an insurmountable
mountain of pain, regret, humiliation, or loss quite
suddenly and literally disappears. Such depth is
there to universal truth, that we have no suitable
concept. Listen to your bursting, Universal heart.
Feel the freedom of complete truth coursing
through the veins of all that you conceive.

Meditate on the unnecessary, and futile
task of grasping eternity. Know its completeness
without need of thought, as you soar freely through
the infinite depths. Do not worry with
understanding. Letting it be, as it is, will always
suffice.

Laugh lovingly at the realization that the
Universe of truth is forever expanding. Feel its
rhythm joyously, and know that it is always
changing. Comprehend that all communicable
knowledge is nothing more than an arrow shot
toward the moon. Watch as the arrow disappears

into the darkness, and allow the Universe to take it from there.

The idea that you are a separate entity, or an island unto yourself, surrounded by a sea of apathy must be vanquished before the light of eternal oneness. As soon as you know yourself to be manifested, your work is done. Simply surrender to your manifestations, and allow them to be. Follow their lead without resistance, and realize the oneness of Universal flow.

Without such an awakening to the fact of I Am; that you are one with the Universe, you will continue to falsely believe yourself contained by ego. You may witness despairing elderly clinging desperately upon their egoic limitations. It may indeed take the passing away from this physical shell to finally dispel the illusion.

What an awakening it must be to "die" to your physical body, and realize that you have

actually been here with or without it all along! Of
course that all happens here and now as well.
There is no reason to swim in illusion.

Let go of the concept that you must create
anything. Understand that everything is now, and
is complete. There is no creation; only
manifestation. What you may imagine yourself
creating is without exception already here awaiting
your attention. Concepts that we are incapable of
imagining are right here, in infinite and abundant
supply.

The ego, through groupthink, may observe,
measure, calculate, and state as "incontrovertible
scientific fact," it's aptly labeled double blind peer
reviewed research. Society knows it's
illusions intimately. Of course these "facts" are
dispersed immediately upon revelation.

Through illusion the ego see truth as a
reflection of itself, instead of itself as a reflection

of truth. The truth does not care about fictions like war, or money, or football games. The truth only begets the truth! Misunderstandings, that's all that's holding us back... as foolish as it sounds, misunderstandings.

These bodies are like instruments. Power is no more found in our bones, and brains, than it is in our guitars, or our hammers. The power, the only power, is in truth. It's right here, right now. We don't need to build it because it is already all that is. We are truth, and death is but a dream. The Truth is neither behind you, nor in front of you. It is here. now, with you, and it's all you need to know.

Incorrect assumptions build their own prison around the thinker. Of course the metaphorical concrete and bars of this ego based prison are only there as long as you allow them to be. You are the key to vanquish any such limitations, or barriers to the abundance this unfathomable universe provides.

Metacognition serves only up to the doorway of letting go. Once through that threshold of surrender, you are home. Our three dimensional perception of "reality" is foreign to the real. Opening up to that which is the source, and depth, of your true being (ultimate surrender) allows truth to bypass reason, and thus spread joy throughout that which is no longer believed to be a void. The fullness of absolute abundance immediately overwhelms frail illusion.

"Reality is merely an illusion, albeit a very persistent one."

- **Albert Einstein**

Chapter 13
-Physics-

The most enlightened physicist must also check his or her ego at the door. Measuring, quantifying, and "proving," may, or may not have anything to do with what actually is. A scientist operating free of ego understands that science is not absolute. Science has limitations. We simply do not know what we do not know. Physics may delve into the mystery of being, but it is inept to provide absolute answers.

Einstein did not simply stand in front of his desk and wait for the Universe to magically send information. He understood that the information was already there, in perfect form. Everything that he discovered was already in existence. He understood that he had nothing to create, and certainly nothing to teach the Universe. He was a believer in intuition, and knew that his place was to find the flow within the Universe, which has always been established, and available.

Physics, like other scientific fields, provide us with beauty (not unlike music and art). However, a blind faith in our current scientific understanding is nearly as short sighted as operating under the tyranny of iron clad religious dogma. A healthy agnosticism (free of egoic groupthink) is key to navigating both fields.

Science which is free from ego will certainly not conclude based upon a lack of evidence that something is, or is not so. Confidently declaring that a lack of evidence proves anything scientifically is clearly unscientific. Allowing what is, to be, is not unscientific.

There are physicists in our culture who claim that they have solved the riddle regarding the origins of the Universe. They propagate a theory which proves everything. This is pure ego parading as science. The statements they make have no more validity than absolutes spouted from a religious pulpit.

The more anything is discovered, the more vast becomes the space of the unknown. Every answered question inevitably yields new questions not previously considered. Science is beautiful, strong, and limited.

"The whole
universe is
contained within a
single human being
—you."

-Rumi

Chapter 14
-Manifestation-

Manifestations align through feeling, and intrinsically knowing. Even though this is an effortless process for your true self, it can pose quite a challenge if you are living through the ego. The ego thrives on stories of lack, or past hurt. These are often referred to as "your story." These are not your story.

What you manifest always, and infinitely, resides within you. Simply awaken to its presence and welcome it as part of who you eternally are. Your true heart will awaken, and cast aside false, lustful wishes of the ego. Allow them to dissipate while you recall and revel in the splendor of the true manifestations of your heart.

Through the accepted societal norms and groupthink, it is easy to become numb to the power

of manifestation inherent within you. The illusory
scourge of the fanciful dreamer is one of the more
humorous paradoxes of limiting societal influence
bent on suppression, and adherence to norms.
Instead of encouraging harmony with the true song
of spirit, this powerless shadow attempts to hold
back awakening. The time, as always, is now to
cast it aside.

Taking the face value shallow illusory view
delivered as "that's the way it is...," or the like, is
sufficient only to ride the carousel of false belief
around and around in comfortable slumber. The
literal minded habit of believing everything that
we have been taught to think, is ripe for exposure
as delusion.

Reality awaits the insightful who have
finally had enough.

A universal manifestation is not a gift. It is
an acceptance. To manifest you must first
surrender the false notion that you are in a state of

lack. Under no circumstance will you manifest while swimming under the ice of delusion. To manifest is to know with surrendered certainty that you are one with all that is. This, of course, means that you are already one with all that you truly wish to manifest.

If your ego is deluding you into a false feeling of lack, it will block any true manifestation from entering your awareness. As long as you operate in this egoic pattern, you will continue a dramatic performance of never enough. You can break free from this as soon as you are ready to surrender the story, and see yourself as you truly are: Abundant.

You may wish to manifest freedom. Before you take to your journal and write your desire for freedom, ask yourself what it is from which you wish to gain this freedom. Do you wish to be free from work? From poverty through the collection of money? From entrapment under an oppressor? Freedom from fear?

These wishes indicate a desire to be
somewhere other than where you are right here and
now. This freedom that you wish to manifest
represents an unhappy attachment to your current
circumstance. Like a marble that continues its
momentum round and round the same circular
track, you may feel stuck in a groove; and unsure
how to change course. To remain in this groove is
your choice. The choice to resist going in circles
in the groove is yours. The choice to accept and
embrace your place in the groove is yours. The
choice to detach yourself from the groove and roll
in an entirely new direction is also yours. Either
way, an abstract grasping towards an illusory
concept of freedom is forever fruitless.

Freedom is always yours, and requires no
manifestation. Like the sun, freedom is infinitely
available over the clouds of illusion. You may
"selflessly" wish to manifest peace among others
engaged in warfare. Recognize immediately that
such a wish is a clever attempt of the ego to bring

the other in line with its superior knowledge. The "greater good" is viewed as neither great, nor good, by the perfect Universe.

Busyness confronting, and corralling those in conflict is a splendid sport for those swimming in self righteous delusion. When confronted by such grand egoic temptations, simply bring forth your ability to separate that ego from yourself, and welcome it as a guest. Congratulate the ego on its cleverness, and allow it to play on while you observe its creative antics.

When you are ready to uncover the peace that your ego was hilariously attempting to instill in others, simply sit quietly. Find that peace resides within you; not apart from anything. The Universe is peace, and the universe is you. You and what the ego labels, the warring other, are one. The only one.

You may wish to manifest joy into your every breath. Contemplate the joy of your life. You will find that each moment of joy was hard

earned through the sacrifice of ego; wrenched open
to the light to reveal the lack of nothing.

Joy is the dismissal of that which is not.
The ego clutches tight, and will attempt to drown
you in illusion. In an effort to break through, your
true self may require egoic demise which brings
you a tortuous feeling of implosion, and pain.

You may wish to manifest love. To love is
not to preserve. To love is to rejoice, and release.
There is no possession in love. There is no control
in love. Love is acceptance, surrender, and
respect. The ego wishes to love an ideal; a
projection of what it has invented in illusion. True
love carries no such expectation, and requires only
the ability to let go. Love will then remain,
unconfined and free.

Peace of mind is not contained beneath the
skull. Peace of mind is the radiant, perfect,
vibrational energy of true being. It is an infinite
manifestation of light, truth, and love. Unyielding,

limitless, metaphysical power is happily here upon awakening.

Aspiration is devotion, and you risk nothing by entrusting the Universe with your desires. Allow your aspirations the space to become astral, and elevated. They will then naturally return to you as manifestations.

To find your flow, you must first understand your place as a reflection of the Universe. As a reflection of the Universe you are a piece of eternity, all of your desires will merge into the one and only source through detachment from the ego.

How ridiculous it is to simply tell the Universe what we need, before finding our flow within it. The Universe is the infinite, all encompassing, truth. What information could we possibly provide to this source? Wishing and waiting for superfluous gifts is an exercise in vanity. Instead, understand that gratitude for our perfect place as a reflection of the Universe is the

foundation to establish before finding the flow
necessary to receive more. Insincerity is fatal to
manifestation. Sincere gratitude, motivated by
nothing more than intrinsic joy, will never cease to
manifest blessings.

Manifestation begins in the silent, solitary
seeking of understanding. Sincere gratitude, and
acceptance through inspired actions, brings us in
line with the flow of the Universe. An insincere
desire, born of nothing more than lust will never
rise to flow.

Projecting human-like qualities onto the
Universe is a grave mistake. The Universe makes
no considerations, or judgements based upon
human actions. The Universe simply is waiting for
any and all who discover it's flow. There is no
favoritism, and there are no shortcuts.
When flow is reached and maintained in daily life
it is possible to reach atonement (at-one-ment)
with the Universe.

This at-one-ment is an understanding that I Am the Universe. The universe is mind, and there is only one. This knowing will unceasingly lead to harmonious manifestation.

Decide what it is that your heart desires, then discipline yourself with private focus and perception of it already being so. This alone, however, is insufficient to bring your manifestations into being. Constantly striving and acting as an inspired participant, and coconspirator with the Universe is key to joining the flow. In this way the Universe will assist you in sorting through (discarding) your flights of fancy, and sharpening your focus on the true manifestations of your heart.

No wishing, praying, journaling, poster making, etc. will bring about the manifestations of your heart. It is far simpler than that, yet it requires surrender of the ego. The Universe never bends towards your wishes. The Universe is as it infinitely is. Your perception is the key to unlocking its abundance. And to perceive its abundance you simply need to surrender, become, and be.

Therefore wishing, waiting, wanting, expecting, dreaming, scheming, struggling, stealing, pretending, faking, etc. will never bring about manifestation. Reading, writing, repeating, and praying, are always grossly insufficient to manifest your true heartfelt desires. Activism, legislation, marching, and shouting will not bring you the satisfaction you seek.

Manifestation lies entirely within our grasp. Manifestation is not a dream somewhere out there in the ether waiting four us to magic our way up and grab. Neither is manifestation the process of magnetizing ourselves through our human ego to attract that which is outside of us. Manifestation is not dreaming up luxuries and stating our desire to have them out loud; nor is manifestation writing our luxury, or relationship dreams in a journal a prescribed number of times each day.

Manifestation is the awakening to the power of I Am within. Through this awakening you will find it impossible not to manifest the true desires of your heart (the life of your dreams).

Feeling, and knowing, from the infinite depths of your heart is the only way. There is no course, or curriculum, to reach such a point. You are born into this world as a continuation, and an inseparable part of perfection... which we describe as the Universe.

Surrender, or letting go of resistance, is the key to remembering your place in eternity. Your place is the only place. You are not just part of the Universe; you are the Universe. The secret is that there is no Universe without you, and you are infinite. Silence the ego and unlock manifestation with these words:

I Am the Universe.

Dear Reader,

Thank you for reading <u>The Secret of Universal Manifestation and Abundance</u>. It was a true pleasure to write. If you enjoyed the book I would like to ask that you kindly provide a positive review so that others may find and benefit from the book as well.

Sincerely,
Jack Marshall

Made in the USA
Monee, IL
03 November 2022

17053287R00059